Randy
Orton

ATLANTA FALCONS

TODAY

JOHN NICHOLS

Published by Creative Education
123 South Broad Street, Mankato, Minnesota 56001
Creative Education is an imprint of The Creative Company

Designed by Rita Marshall

Photos by: Allsport USA, AP/Wide World Photos, SportsChrome

Library of Congress Cataloging-in-Publication Data

Nichols, John, 1966–
Atlanta Falcons / by John Nichols.
p. cm. — (NFL today)
Summary: Traces the history of the team from its beginnings through 1999.
ISBN 1-58341-035-X

1. Atlanta Falcons (Football team)—History—Juvenile literature. [1. Atlanta
Falcons (Football team)—History. 2. Football—History.] I. Title. II. Series: NFL
today (Mankato, Minn.)

GV956.A85N53   2000
796.332'64'09758231—dc21   99-015739

First edition

9 8 7 6 5 4 3 2 1

In the Southeast, all roads lead to Atlanta, or at least it seems that way. Atlanta, the capital of Georgia, is one of the largest cities in the South. It is also the hub of the region, a focal point of business and culture.

Atlanta was the jewel of the South before the Civil War. In those days, all railroads led to Atlanta. Then, during the war, the city was nearly burned to the ground and the rail lines were destroyed. It was Union General William T. Sherman's plan to force the Confederacy to surrender, which it eventually did. But after the war, the people of Atlanta rebuilt their city into an impressive metropolitan center.

Defensive end Claude Humphrey terrorized quarterbacks.

1 9 6 5

Atlanta's team was officially named the Falcons, after the swift birds, on August 24.

Given its rich history, it is not surprising that Atlanta is home to the oldest National Football League team in the South. The Atlanta Falcons began playing in 1966, becoming the 15th team in the NFL. The club was an instant financial success and topped the headlines in sports pages throughout the region. It was a hit everywhere—except on the field.

The Falcons have struggled in most of their years in the league, yet Atlanta fans have continued to support their team. They have applauded the efforts of defensive stars such as Tommy Nobis, Claude Humphrey, Deion Sanders, and Jessie Tuggle. They've also seen some spectacular offense from standouts such as Steve Bartkowski, William Andrews, Gerald Riggs, Andre Rison, and Jamal Anderson. After finally reaching the Super Bowl in 1998, today's Falcons look ready to soar to championship heights.

NOBIS KNOCKS HEADS

The Falcons didn't fly very high in their first few years in the NFL, but they did pound opposing offenses. In the beginning, the Atlanta franchise was built mainly around its defense. The first player the team chose in the 1966 college draft was a hard-nosed linebacker from the University of Texas named Tommy Nobis. The Falcons needed Nobis, but first they had to convince him to play in Atlanta.

In those days, there were two professional football leagues, the NFL and the AFL (American Football League). The Houston Oilers team in the AFL also wanted to sign Nobis. One Oilers fan, astronaut Frank Boorman, even made a pitch from space to try to convince the young Texan to

The anchor of the Falcons defense, linebacker Jessie Tuggle.

1 9 6 6

Rookie linebacker Tommy Nobis made an incredible 296 total tackles.

stay in his home state. But Nobis finally decided to accept the challenge of playing with the first-year Falcons instead.

What the Falcons got was a player who enjoyed the challenge of defense. Nobis once explained his basic approach: "I hit 'em right in the goozle—high and hard. That way they don't go anywhere but down."

Nobis led the Falcons' defense like a one-man wrecking crew. "He was great long before the Atlanta Falcons were good," one football writer explained. "An expansion team, the Falcons were stocked mostly with free agents and castoffs from other clubs. Nobis was virtually a one-man defense."

Unfortunately, Nobis couldn't play both defense and offense. Quarterback Randy Johnson, running back Junior Coffey, and end Alex Hawkins tried their best, but the team scored 20 or more points only four times all season in 1966. Despite its hard work and optimism, Atlanta finished with a dismal 3–11 record.

The Falcons fell flat on their tail feathers in the 1967 season as well, winning only one game. Typically, Nobis played a big role in that victory. Atlanta was trailing the Minnesota Vikings 20–14 when Nobis recovered a fumble and rumbled with the ball deep into Minnesota territory. From there, Randy Johnson guided the Falcons to a touchdown and a 21–20 win.

The following year, the Falcons changed coaches and drafted another defensive star. The new coach was former pro quarterback Norm Van Brocklin. The new defensive standout was lineman Claude Humphrey from Tennessee State.

Humphrey was as tough as Nobis and perhaps even more self-confident. During an early-season game against the first-place Baltimore Colts, Humphrey stared at All-Pro quarterback Johnny Unitas and growled, "I'm going to run you out of the league." That was pretty tough talk for a mere rookie. Humphrey, though, backed up his words with a series of ferocious hits on the Colts' quarterback. The Colts won, 28–20, but Humphrey quickly established himself as one of the league's most dominant defenders.

By 1969, Van Brocklin's coaching system began to take effect, and the Falcons' defense, led by Nobis, Humphrey, end John Zook, and cornerback Ken Reaves, battered opponents. The Falcons won their last three games to finish at 6–8, their best record yet. They also found a new star that year: powerful rookie center Jeff Van Note out of Kentucky. Van Note began a string of 18 seasons with the Falcons in 1969. By the time he retired in 1986, Van Note had set new franchise records for total games played (246) and consecutive games played (155).

The Falcons continued to improve under Van Brocklin. In 1971, they recorded their first winning season at 7–6–1. They ended the 1972 campaign at 7–7. The defense was clicking on all cylinders, but the offense continued to sputter. In the final game of the 1972 season, running back Dave Hampton was on the verge of making history as the first Atlanta runner to rush for more than 1,000 yards in a season. When Hampton achieved that goal, officials stopped the game and awarded him the ball. Unfortunately, Hampton carried the ball once more. This time he was thrown for a five-yard loss, leaving his rushing total at only 995 yards at the game's end. Hampton kept the game ball but lost the record. He finally broke the 1,000-yard barrier for good in 1975.

1 9 7 2

Dave Hampton set a new franchise record in yards per carry (4.3).

Star quarterback Steve Bartkowski.

Bruising running back Gerald Riggs.

The Falcons seemed ready to achieve another milestone in 1973—reaching the playoffs for the first time. After a slow start, the club won seven straight games to climb to 8–3 and needed just two wins in the last three contests to secure a postseason berth. However, back-to-back losses to Buffalo and St. Louis ended the year on a sour note.

Everything fell apart for Atlanta in 1974. First, the team went on a losing streak, costing Van Brocklin his coaching job. He was replaced at midseason by assistant Marion Campbell. Then the fans lost heart. At the last home game of the season, nearly 49,000 seats in Atlanta-Fulton County Stadium were empty. Atlanta needed a hero.

BRING ON BARTKOWSKI

The next season, out of the West rode a 6-foot-4 and 215-pound quarterback named Steve Bartkowski. Atlanta had traded several players and draft picks to get the number one pick in the 1975 NFL draft. With it, they chose Bartkowski, an All-American out of the University of California.

Fans throughout the Southeast expected big improvements, and Bartkowski didn't mind the attention. In fact, he loved it. "I enjoyed picking up the paper and reading that I was the savior," Bartkowski said. "I really thought I could walk in here and turn this team around overnight."

However, injuries and mistakes set Bartkowski's timetable to stardom back considerably. He had trouble adjusting to pro defenses and suffered through a tough 4–10 campaign his rookie year. He then missed much of the following two seasons with knee injuries.

In 1978, Bartkowski returned, healthy at last and determined to prove himself on the field. But a miserable showing in a preseason game led new coach Leeman Bennett to bench the young quarterback. In the locker room after the game, Bartkowski sat and cried. "That was the lowest I've ever been in my life," he recalled, "and it was the best thing that ever happened to me."

Bartkowski, who loved fast cars and late nights, turned his life around and became deeply religious. He was determined to become a better person and a leader for the Falcons. "I have a motto: If you don't stand for something, you'll fall for anything," he said.

Bartkowski regained his starting job before the fifth game of the 1978 season and led the team on a seven-game win-

Wide receiver Alfred Jenkins caught 41 passes for 710 yards and six touchdowns.

Rolland Lawrence anchored the secondary in the '70s.

13

ning streak that put it in the playoffs for the first time in franchise history with a 9–7 record. Then, in a first-round game against the Philadelphia Eagles, Bartkowski keyed a fourth-quarter rally, tossing two touchdown passes to turn a 13–0 deficit into an exciting 14–13 victory.

Atlanta fans began dreaming a little, with their Falcons just two steps away from the Super Bowl. The following week in Dallas, however, reality struck. The Falcons fought valiantly against the powerful Cowboys, but Dallas held on for a 27–20 win, ending Atlanta's best year yet.

1 9 7 9

Wallace Francis became the first Falcons receiver to gain 1,000 yards in a season.

ANDREWS RUSHES IN

The next season didn't bring the Falcons a Super Bowl berth either, but it did mark the arrival of the team's next star: running back William Andrews. During his college career at Auburn, Andrews spent most of his time blocking for teammate Joe Cribbs, a future star for the Buffalo Bills. At first, Coach Bennett planned to use Andrews primarily to block for another rookie runner, Lynn Cain. But Andrews looked so good in the preseason that Bennett decided to give him the ball.

Andrews made the coach look brilliant by rushing for more than 100 yards in each of his first two regular-season games with Atlanta. By the end of the year, Andrews had set a new team rushing record with 1,023 yards. He achieved his success with a unique style: running slightly bent over with his head lowered. "I try to stay lower than my opponent," Andrews once explained, "come at him in a ball, and then . . . pow!"

14   *Like Andrews, Chris Miller was a team leader.*

Record-setting halfback William Andrews.

Andrews topped his outstanding rookie season with an even better year in 1980. He rushed for more than 1,300 yards and caught passes for 736 more. Few running backs had ever contributed more than 2,000 total yards in one season. With Andrews leading the way on the ground and Bartkowski having his best year as a pro, the Falcons went 12–4 in 1980, captured the NFL's Western Division title, and earned a first-round bye in the playoffs.

In the second round, the Falcons faced off once more against the Dallas Cowboys. This time, Atlanta was determined to get revenge. Bartkowski tossed touchdown passes to Andrews and speedy receiver Alfred Jenkins, and Cain rushed for a third score to power Atlanta to a 27–17 lead midway through the fourth quarter.

Then the Cowboys took over. Dallas quarterback Danny White hit All-Pro receiver Drew Pearson with two late game touchdown strikes for a 31–27 Cowboys win. Atlanta's best season ever was over too early, but hopes were high that even better times were ahead.

The rest of the early 1980s, however, did not prove kind to the Falcons or their fans. Although the club's offense, featuring Bartkowski, Andrews, and Jenkins, was now strong, its defense was suspect. Bartkowski set club records in 1981 with 297 completions for 3,830 yards. His chief target was Jenkins, who led the NFL with 70 catches for 1,358 yards and 13 touchdowns.

Andrews also seemed to get better and better. He played in the Pro Bowl four straight years, from 1980 to 1983. Andrews was one of the best players on the field, but he was also one of the best citizens off the field, devoting much of

1 9 8 1

Safety Tom Pridemore returned seven interceptions for 221 yards—a Falcons record.

The first Falcons teams were known for their defense (pages 18-19).

17

Halfback John Settle was named to the Pro Bowl after gaining 1,594 all-purpose yards.

his time to charity work. Andrews always had a smile and a positive outlook in almost any situation. "William Andrews can catch fish even when they won't bite," said Atlanta defensive coach Tommy Brasher.

Andrews needed all of his positive thinking in 1984. During a preseason scrimmage, he was tackled from behind and heard a snap in his knee. As it turned out, both the knee and the muscles around it were badly damaged. Andrews sat out two seasons and went through endless hours of painful physical therapy to re-strengthen the knee.

When he finally returned in 1986, the Falcons and their fans greeted him as a hero. But this hero wasn't what he used to be. Soon after his attempt at a comeback, Andrews retired as Atlanta's all-time leading rusher.

"PRIME TIME" ARRIVES IN ATLANTA

Losing Andrews set back the Falcons' progress in the mid-1980s, though several exciting new players tried to pick up the slack. Gerald Riggs, who arrived in 1982 from Arizona State, quickly established himself as an All-Pro runner. He averaged nearly 1,000 yards per season in his seven years in Atlanta, including a club-record 1,719 yards in 1985.

Wide receiver and kick returner Billy Johnson was another Atlanta favorite during his years with the Falcons. Johnson was known as "White Shoes" because of his bright footwear. Opponents hated watching those white shoes race by in a blur when Johnson returned punts and kickoffs.

Despite the efforts of Riggs, Johnson, and Bartkowski, the Falcons recorded one losing season after another in the

1980s. Coach Bennett gave way to Dan Henning in 1983, and Marion Campbell returned for a second stint at the Atlanta helm in 1987. Each tried, unsuccessfully, to find a winning combination.

In the late 1980s, two important draft picks keyed another rebuilding effort in Atlanta. The first was Chris Miller, drafted out of Oregon in 1987 to assume the team's quarterbacking duties. Miller's strong arm and leadership abilities provided some hope for the future on offense, but the Atlanta defense was still weak. To help remedy that, the Falcons chose Florida State defensive back Deion Sanders in the first round of the 1989 NFL draft. Sanders was flashy and talented, earning him two nicknames—"Neon Deion" and "Prime Time."

It appeared at first, however, that Atlanta wouldn't be able

Quarterback Chris Miller had an outstanding season, throwing for 3,459 total yards.

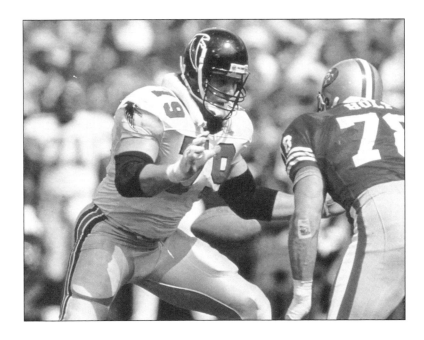

22   *Deion Sanders had speed to spare as a cornerback and punt returner.*

to sign the brilliant cornerback. Sanders and his agent made it clear that the Falcons would have to pay the young star a fortune or lose him to his other love—baseball. While in college, Sanders spent his summers playing baseball in the New York Yankees organization, and the Yankees were willing to pay Deion generously. But Sanders had an alternative plan in mind. He figured he could play both sports—baseball in the summer and football in the fall.

Sanders tried it in 1989. While his agent and the Falcons tried to work out a contract, Deion played for the Yankees. One night in Seattle, he hit a home run and then returned to the dugout, where he received a phone call saying that Atlanta had offered a multimillion-dollar contract. One inning after hitting a homer, Sanders said goodbye to his Yankees teammates and rushed to the airport to catch a plane to Atlanta. The next day, he was on the Falcons' practice field.

In his first regular-season game with the Falcons, Sanders proved what a weapon he was. Against the Los Angeles Rams, he caught a punt and then dropped it. With Rams tacklers bearing down on him, Sanders calmly picked up the ball, raced to his right, broke several tackles, and went 70 yards for a touchdown. "In 27 years in the league, I've never experienced the buzz that goes through a stadium when this guy gets near the football," Coach Campbell said.

Miller and Sanders were soon joined in Atlanta by wide receiver Andre Rison, who came over in a trade with the Indianapolis Colts. Atlanta also brought in a new coach—Jerry Glanville, who had previously helped build the Houston Oilers into a winner. Glanville was an eccentric leader who dressed completely in black and left tickets at the box office

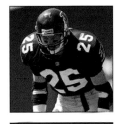

1 9 9 0

Hard-hitting safety Scott Case tied for the team lead with three interceptions.

each home game for Elvis Presley, just in case the deceased singer was really still alive, as some of his fans believed.

Glanville changed the team's jerseys from red to black. He also changed the team's attitude. Using a high-powered "Red Gun" offense developed by assistant coach June Jones, Glanville helped turn the Falcons into one of the league's most exciting clubs.

Head coach Jerry Glanville's Falcons averaged more than 30 points in each victory.

REEVES TO THE RESCUE

In the early '90s, the Falcons experienced moderate success under the guidance of Coach Glanville. In 1991, they put together a 10–6 mark and advanced to the second round of the playoffs. Unfortunately, they fell to the Washington

Andre Rison led the Falcons in receiving for four seasons.

Redskins, who would go on to win the Super Bowl. The next season, the team slumped back to 6–10, and Atlanta's colorful coach was fired.

June Jones took over the coaching duties in 1994 and maneuvered the Falcons back into Super Bowl contention. Quarterback Jeff George and receiver Terance Mathis, both new additions to the team, led Atlanta to a 9–7 record and a playoff berth in 1995. Unfortunately, the Falcons had to travel to frigid Green Bay, where the Packers thumped them 37–20 in a snowy battle.

Falcons fans took consolation in the hopes of continued success, but 1996 proved to be disastrous. Jeff George struggled early in the season, and when Coach Jones removed him from a game, the quarterback and the coach got into a heated argument. George was suspended, and Atlanta stumbled to a 3–13 record. At the end of the season, Jones was fired and George was released. The Falcons seemed to be at rock bottom again.

Fortunately for Atlanta, positive change was coming. On January 20, 1997, the Falcons named Dan Reeves their new head coach. Reeves had been a successful coach with the Denver Broncos and the New York Giants, leading both teams to the playoffs and Denver to three Super Bowl appearances. "To get a coach of Dan's caliber in here gives us hope," said defensive end Chuck Smith. "He's a winner and he knows what it takes to get it done in this league."

One of Reeves's first moves was to acquire veteran Chris Chandler from the Houston Oilers to shore up the quarterback position. Still, halfway through the 1997 season, the Falcons' record stood at 1–7. But sparked by Chandler's

1 9 9 5

End Chris Doleman made nine sacks and was named to his seventh Pro Bowl game.

Swift and crafty receiver Terance Mathis (pages 26-27).

sharp passing and an increasingly feisty defense, Atlanta reeled off six wins in its last eight contests to finish 7–9. Reeves's winning spirit had begun to rub off on his team, and it seemed that better days were ahead.

1997

Receiver Bert Emanuel pulled in 65 passes for nine touchdowns and nearly 1,000 yards.

THE "DIRTY BIRDS"

One player who was key in the Falcons' resurgence was a stocky running back picked up in the seventh round of the 1994 draft. At 5-foot-11 and 235 pounds, Jamal Anderson was considered by many NFL scouts to be a "tweener"—too big to be a halfback and too small to be a blocking fullback. But the confident University of Utah product had little doubt that he could succeed in the NFL.

After waiting on the bench for two years behind veteran back Craig "Ironhead" Heyward, Anderson proved to be a rising star for Atlanta in 1996, rushing for 1,066 yards and making a big impression on incoming coach Dan Reeves. "Jamal's going to be a big part of our offense," Coach Reeves said. "He's going to be our guy."

In 1998, Anderson and the Falcons were looking to build on their strong '97 finish. "It's time to stand up and be counted," said cornerback Ray Buchanan. "No more rebuilding and moral victories. It's time to get it done." Armed with Anderson's strong running and Chris Chandler's pinpoint passing, the Falcons' physical offense left lumps on the opposition. Anderson ran for 1,846 yards and 14 touchdowns on an NFL-record 410 carries.

During his record-setting season, Anderson also created a touchdown dance to help fire up his team. After scoring, he would hop from one foot to the other while flapping his arms like wings. "The Dirty Bird," as he named the dance, became the Falcons' rallying cry as they soared to a 14–2 record and captured the NFC West title.

In the playoffs, Atlanta beat San Francisco 20–18 to advance to the NFC championship game against the 16–1 Vikings in Minnesota. Atlanta was a heavy underdog, and early on, it appeared that Minnesota would run away with the game. Near the end of the first half, the Vikings led 20–7 and were threatening to score again when Atlanta defensive end Chuck Smith stripped the ball from Vikings quarterback Randall Cunningham and Atlanta recovered. The turnover set up a Chandler to Terance Mathis touchdown pass that revived the Dirty Birds.

Speedy Tim Dwight averaged more than 20 yards per catch and starred as a kick returner.

Fearsome pass-rushing end Chuck Smith.

Jamal Anderson ran with both power and finesse.

One of the league's finest cornerbacks, Ray Buchanan.   31

The Falcons faithful expected speedy receiver Shawn Jefferson to add to Atlanta's air attack.

In the second half, Atlanta gained momentum, and at the end of regulation, the score stood tied at 27–27. In overtime, the Falcons' defense held the Vikings' powerful offense twice before Atlanta marched down the field and kicker Morten Andersen booted a 38-yard field goal to win the game. The once-lowly Falcons were Super Bowl-bound at last.

In the Super Bowl, the Falcons met the defending champion Denver Broncos. Atlanta took the first lead at 3–0, but Denver stormed back with its potent offense to win 34–19. "It's disappointing, but we lost to a fine team," said Chandler. "I guess our time is yet to come."

Unfortunately, the momentum built in 1998 would be lost the next season to injuries. In the second game of the year, Anderson took a handoff, tried to cut sharply, and fell to the ground with a season-ending knee injury. The next week, Chandler was also sidelined by a leg injury. Stripped of their two offensive stars, the Falcons sputtered to a 5–11 record. "We're better than that—a lot better," a frustrated Coach Reeves said. "This is a step backward, but I believe this team still has what it takes to be a winner."

With the healthy return of their stars and the addition of such players as receiver Shawn Jefferson and cornerback Ashley Ambrose, the future looks bright for Atlanta in the new century. After finally earning their first conference championship, these high-flying Falcons are eager to return to their perch atop the NFC.